# Ghosts of Paris: Ten Haunted Places in the City of Love

Edward Turner

Published by Oliver Lancaster, 2023.

GHOSTS OF PARIS: TEN HAUNTED PLACES IN THE CITY OF LOVE

**First edition. July 7, 2023.**

Copyright © 2023 Edward Turner.

ISBN: 979-8215161166

Written by Edward Turner.

# Also by Edward Turner

Ghosts of Paris: Ten Haunted Places in the City of Love

# Ghosts of Paris:

# Ten Haunted Places in the City of Love

# GHOSTS OF PARIS: TEN HAUNTED PLACES IN THE CITY OF LOVE

# Introduction

Paris, the City of Love, has captured the hearts of millions around the world. Its picturesque landmarks, enchanting ambiance, and rich cultural heritage have made it one of the most popular tourist destinations globally. However, beneath the surface of this stunning city lies a dark and intriguing side that is rarely talked about. Paris is not only known for its artistic and cultural contributions but also for its gruesome history, revolution, and bloodshed. Over the years, many legends and tales of haunted places have been passed down through generations, adding to the city's mystique and allure. In this book, we will explore ten of the most rumoured haunted places in Paris, delving into their history and the ghosts that are said to haunt them.

Ghost stories have always been an essential part of the world's folklore, captivating the imagination and drawing people in. The ghosts of Paris are no exception. The tales of haunted places have been passed down through generations, adding to the city's allure and mystique. Whether you're a believer in the paranormal or not, the ghost stories of Paris have a way of captivating the imagination.

Paris has been an inspiration for artists, writers, and thinkers for centuries. Its romantic allure has inspired some of the most haunting works of art, literature, and music. Yet, beneath its beauty lies a dark history that has seen its fair share of bloodshed, revolution, and tragedy. It is no wonder that Paris is rumoured to be one of the most haunted cities in the world.

This book takes you on a journey to some of the most notorious and haunted locations in Paris. The chapters are arranged chronologically, taking you through the city's haunted history. The journey begins in the catacombs, the underground ossuaries that hold the remains of millions of Parisians. The catacombs were created in the late 18th century when the city's cemeteries were overflowing with bodies. The catacombs have become a macabre tourist attraction, with tourists visiting to see the skulls and bones arranged in elaborate patterns.

Moving on, we explore the iconic Opera Garnier, which is said to be haunted by the Phantom of the Opera. The story of the Phantom has become a part of Parisian folklore, and many believe that the ghost still haunts the opera house. We then delve into the Père Lachaise Cemetery, the final resting place of some of the most famous and influential figures in French history. The cemetery is rumoured to be haunted by the ghosts of some of its famous residents, including Jim Morrison, Oscar Wilde, Edith Piaf, Frédéric Chopin, and Molière.

Continuing our journey, we explore the Hôtel de Sens, an ancient building that has been a witness to some of Paris's most significant events. The building is said to be haunted by the ghost of a former resident who was murdered in the building. We then move on to the Hôtel de Ville, where the ghosts of the executed are said to haunt the halls. The building has seen its fair share of bloodshed, and the ghosts of the executed are said to roam the halls.

# GHOSTS OF PARIS: TEN HAUNTED PLACES IN THE CITY OF LOVE

Moving on, we visit the Palace of Versailles, a place that was once the seat of power for the French monarchy. The palace is rumoured to be haunted by the ghosts of Marie Antoinette and Louis XVI, who were executed during the French Revolution. The ghosts of the former monarchs are said to roam the halls of the palace, haunting visitors to this day.

Continuing our journey, we explore the Château de Châteaubriant, a mediaeval castle that has been the scene of some of the most gruesome events in French history. The castle is said to be haunted by the ghosts of its former residents, who were brutally murdered during the Hundred Years War. We also visit the infamous La Conciergerie, a former prison that was used during the French Revolution to hold prisoners before they were executed. The prison is said to be haunted by the ghosts of those who died within its walls, and visitors have reported feeling an eerie presence within the building.

Next, we delve into the story of the Hôtel Drouot, a famous auction house that is said to be haunted by the ghosts of its former owners. The building has been witness to some of the most significant auctions in history, and the ghosts of the past are said to linger within its walls.

Moving on, we visit the Musée de la Chasse et de la Nature, a museum dedicated to hunting and nature. The museum is said to be haunted by the ghost of a young woman who died tragically in the building. Visitors have reported feeling a presence within the museum and have even seen the ghostly apparition of the young woman.

Our journey through the haunted places of Paris ends at the Parc des Buttes-Chaumont, a beautiful park that is said to be haunted by the ghosts of those who were executed during the Paris Commune. The park has a dark history, and the ghosts of the past are said to roam the park at night.

In this book, we will have explored ten of the most rumoured haunted places in Paris, delving into their history and the ghosts that are said to haunt them. The stories of these haunted places add to the mystique and allure of Paris, making it one of the most fascinating and intriguing cities in the world. Whether you're a believer in the paranormal or not, the ghost stories of Paris have a way of captivating the imagination and drawing you in.

# GHOSTS OF PARIS: TEN HAUNTED PLACES IN THE CITY OF LOVE

# Chapter 1: The Catacombs of Paris

Beneath the bustling streets of Paris lies a macabre underworld that few have seen - the catacombs. These underground tunnels hold the remains of millions of Parisians, dating back centuries. But with such a dark history, it's no surprise that these tunnels are rumoured to be haunted by the ghosts of the past.

## The History and Purpose of the Catacombs

PARIS IS KNOWN FOR its romantic charm, world-class museums, and stunning architecture. But beneath the city's surface lies a darker side of history that few tourists ever get to see. The catacombs of Paris are a maze of underground tunnels and chambers that span over 200 miles beneath the city streets. The catacombs were created in the late 18th century to solve a growing public health problem. At the time, Paris was suffering from a shortage of burial space, and cemeteries were overcrowded, leading to unsanitary conditions and the spread of disease. The solution was to move the remains of millions of Parisians to the abandoned quarries beneath the city.

The catacombs were not designed to be a tourist attraction. In fact, they were initially closed to the public and only accessible to workers responsible for moving the bones. It wasn't until the early 19th century that the catacombs were opened to the public, and even then, they were only accessible by guided tour.

Today, the catacombs are a popular tourist attraction, drawing millions of visitors each year who come to explore the macabre labyrinth of tunnels and learn about the city's history.

## The Legend of the Ghostly Figures that Roam the Catacombs

BUT WITH SUCH A DARK history, it's no surprise that the catacombs have gained a reputation for being haunted. The most famous legend is that of the ghostly figures that are said to roam the tunnels at night. According to the legend, the ghosts are the restless souls of those buried in the catacombs, doomed to wander the tunnels for all eternity.

One of the most famous ghost stories associated with the catacombs is that of Philibert Aspairt, a caretaker who worked in the catacombs in the early 19th century. Legend has it that Aspairt went missing one day while working in the catacombs, and his body was never found. Some believe that his ghost still haunts the catacombs, and visitors have reported seeing a ghostly figure dressed in the 19th century wandering the tunnels.

## Other Rumoured Ghostly Sightings and Experiences

WHILE THE LEGEND OF the ghostly figures is the most famous, it's not the only ghost story associated with the catacombs. Visitors have reported a range of paranormal experiences, including strange noises, unexplained cold spots, and even the feeling of being touched by something unseen.

# GHOSTS OF PARIS: TEN HAUNTED PLACES IN THE CITY OF LOVE

One of the most common experiences reported by visitors is the feeling of being watched or followed. Some have reported hearing whispers or footsteps following them as they make their way through the tunnels. Others have reported feeling as though something is brushing past them or tugging on their clothing.

There have also been reports of unexplained phenomena, such as doors opening and closing on their own, or objects moving without explanation. Some have reported seeing apparitions or shadows moving along the walls of the tunnels.

The catacombs of Paris are a fascinating and eerie place, steeped in history and legend. While the catacombs are now a popular tourist attraction, they remain shrouded in mystery and the subject of numerous ghost stories and legends. Whether or not these stories are true, the catacombs continue to captivate and intrigue visitors from around the world. If you're brave enough to explore the catacombs yourself, be prepared for an experience that is both chilling and unforgettable.

Despite the numerous reports of ghostly sightings and experiences, the catacombs of Paris remain a popular destination for tourists seeking to explore the city's dark past. Visitors can take a guided tour of the tunnels, which includes a visit to the ossuary where the remains of millions of Parisians are stored.

While the catacombs can be a fascinating and eerie place to visit, it's important to remember that they are also a place of great historical significance. As you explore the tunnels and contemplate the stories of the ghosts that are said to haunt them, take a moment to reflect on the lives of the millions of Parisians whose remains now rest within the catacombs. Their stories may be lost to time, but their legacy lives on in the city they once called home.

# GHOSTS OF PARIS: TEN HAUNTED PLACES IN THE CITY OF LOVE

# Chapter 2: The Opera Garnier

The Opera Garnier, also known as the Palais Garnier, is a stunning example of Beaux-Arts architecture located in the heart of Paris. Built in the late 19th century, it remains one of the most famous and well-regarded opera houses in the world. However, beneath its beauty lies a darker side, as the Opera Garnier is also famous for its ghostly sightings and legends. In this chapter, we will explore the history and architecture of the Opera Garnier, the legend of the Phantom of the Opera, and other rumoured ghostly sightings and experiences.

## The History and Architecture of the Opera Garnier

THE OPERA GARNIER WAS commissioned in the 1860s by Napoleon III, who sought to create a grand opera house that would rival the great theatres of Europe. The task of designing the building was given to architect Charles Garnier, who created a masterpiece of Beaux-Arts architecture that is still admired today. The building's exterior is notable for its ornate facade, which features numerous sculptures and a grand staircase leading up to the main entrance. Inside, the theatre is just as impressive, with a large seating area, intricate ceiling frescoes, and a massive chandelier that famously crashed to the ground in 1896, killing one person.

The Opera Garnier has played an important role in Parisian cultural history, hosting countless famous operas, ballets, and other performances over the years. Today, it remains a popular destination for visitors to the city, who come to marvel at its beauty and experience a performance in one of the world's most renowned opera houses.

## The Legend of the Phantom of the Opera

PERHAPS THE MOST FAMOUS ghostly legend associated with the Opera Garnier is that of the Phantom of the Opera. The legend tells the story of a mysterious figure who haunts the theatre, causing mischief and mayhem. According to the legend, the Phantom was a disfigured musical genius who fell in love with a young soprano named Christine. When she rejected his advances, he lashed out by causing accidents and sabotaging performances. The legend has been the basis for numerous adaptations, including Gaston Leroux's novel and the famous musical.

Despite being a work of fiction, the legend of the Phantom of the Opera has captured the public imagination and inspired numerous reported sightings of the ghostly figure. Some visitors to the Opera Garnier claim to have seen the Phantom lurking in the shadows or heard his eerie laughter echoing through the halls. While there is no concrete evidence to support the existence of the Phantom, the legend remains a potent and enduring part of the Opera Garnier's legacy.

## Other Rumoured Ghostly Sightings and

# Experiences

IN ADDITION TO THE legend of the Phantom of the Opera, there are numerous other rumoured ghostly sightings and experiences associated with the Opera Garnier. Some visitors claim to have seen the ghost of a ballet dancer who died in the theatre, while others have reported feeling an eerie presence in certain parts of the building. The theatre's underground lake, which features prominently in the Phantom of the Opera legend, has also been the site of reported paranormal activity.

While it's impossible to say for certain whether these reported sightings and experiences are genuine or simply the product of overactive imaginations, they serve to enhance the Opera Garnier's reputation as a haunted and mysterious place.

The Opera Garnier is a masterpiece of architecture and a testament to Parisian cultural history. However, it is also a place shrouded in mystery and legend, with numerous ghostly sightings and experiences reported over the years. Whether you believe in the paranormal or not, there's no denying that the Opera Garnier has an undeniable air of mystery and intrigue that has captured the public imagination for generations. From the legend of the Phantom of the Opera to the rumoured sightings of other ghosts, the Opera Garnier is a place that continues to fascinate and inspire visitors from around the world. Whether you're a lover of opera and ballet or simply interested in the paranormal, a visit to the Opera Garnier is sure to be an unforgettable experience. As you sit in the theatre and take in its beauty, you may just find yourself wondering if there truly are ghosts lurking in its shadows.

# GHOSTS OF PARIS: TEN HAUNTED PLACES IN THE CITY OF LOVE

# Chapter 3: The Père Lachaise Cemetery

The Père Lachaise Cemetery, located in the 20th arrondissement of Paris, is one of the most famous cemeteries in the world. Established in 1804, it covers an area of 44 hectares and is the final resting place of many notable figures from history, culture, and the arts. From Jim Morrison to Edith Piaf, the cemetery is home to the graves of countless luminaries, each with their own fascinating story to tell.

## Famous Graves of The Père Lachaise Cemetery

AS YOU ENTER THE CEMETERY, you can feel the weight of history and the solemnity of the surroundings. The winding paths lead you through the rows of graves, each one a testament to a life that has passed. Among the famous graves, some of the most notable include:

### Jim Morrison

JIM MORRISON WAS AN American singer, songwriter, and poet who rose to fame as the lead vocalist of the rock band, The Doors. He was born on December 8, 1943, in Melbourne, Florida and attended the University of California, Los Angeles, where he met the other members of the band.

Morrison's charismatic stage presence, poetic lyrics, and controversial behaviour made him a cultural icon of the 1960s counterculture movement. His performances with The Doors, including hits such as "Light My Fire" and "Break On Through (To the Other Side)," were known for their improvisational and sometimes provocative nature.

Morrison died on July 3, 1971, in Paris, France, at the age of 27, leaving behind a legacy as one of the most influential and enigmatic figures in rock and roll history.

## Edith Piaf

EDITH PIAF, BORN EDITH Giovanna Gassion, was a French singer and songwriter who became an international sensation during the mid-20th century. She was born on December 19, 1915, in Belleville, Paris, and grew up in extreme poverty. Her mother was a café singer, and her father was a street performer and circus acrobat who abandoned the family when Edith was still a child.

Despite her difficult upbringing, Edith Piaf found solace in music and began singing on the streets of Paris as a teenager. Her unique voice and emotive performances quickly gained attention, and she was discovered by Louis Leplée, the owner of a popular Parisian cabaret. Leplée gave her the stage name "Piaf," which means "sparrow" in French, and she soon became a regular performer at his club.

In 1936, Edith Piaf recorded her first hit song, "Mon Légionnaire," which became an instant success. She went on to release numerous other popular songs, including "La Vie en

Rose," "Non, Je Ne Regrette Rien," and "Milord." Her songs often reflected the struggles and joys of everyday life, and her raw, emotional performances made her one of the most beloved singers of her time.

Throughout her life, Edith Piaf faced many personal challenges, including addiction to alcohol and drugs, multiple car accidents, and a series of failed relationships. However, she continued to perform and record music until her death in 1963 at the age of 47.

## Oscar Wilde

OSCAR WILDE WAS A RENOWNED Irish writer and playwright who lived during the late 19th century. Born in Dublin in 1854, Wilde attended Trinity College, Dublin and later went on to study at Oxford University where he became well known for his wit and charm.

Wilde is perhaps best known for his witty plays, such as "The Importance of Being Earnest" and "An Ideal Husband," which are still popular today. These plays were famous for their clever dialogue and satirical commentary on Victorian society.

However, Wilde's personal life was not without controversy. He was known for his flamboyant and extravagant lifestyle, and his homosexuality was not accepted in Victorian England. In 1895, he was convicted of homosexual acts and sentenced to two years' hard labor. This experience had a profound impact on Wilde, and he died in poverty and exile in Paris in 1900 at the age of 46.

## Frédéric Chopin

FRÉDÉRIC CHOPIN WAS a Polish composer and pianist who is widely considered one of the most significant figures in Romantic music. He was born in Żelazowa Wola, Poland, in 1810, and began playing piano at a young age.

Chopin's music is known for its delicate and expressive melodies, and his compositions for piano, such as the "Nocturnes" and "Etudes," remain some of the most popular pieces in classical music.

Chopin lived most of his life in Paris, where he became a renowned figure in the city's artistic and cultural scene. He died in 1849 at the age of 39, leaving behind a legacy as one of the greatest pianists and composers of all time.

## Molière

MOLIÈRE, BORN JEAN-Baptiste Poquelin, was a French playwright and actor who is considered one of the greatest figures in Western literature. He was born in Paris in 1622 and began his career as an actor before eventually turning to writing plays.

Molière's works, including "Tartuffe," "The Misanthrope," and "The School for Wives," are known for their biting wit, satire, and criticism of the societal norms of 17th-century France. Despite facing opposition from the French aristocracy and the Catholic Church, Molière's plays were hugely popular and continue to be performed and studied today.

He died in 1673, shortly after collapsing on stage during a performance of his final play, "The Imaginary Invalid."

THESE ARE JUST A FEW of the many famous graves that can be found in Père Lachaise. Each one has its own story to tell, and the cemetery is a testament to the rich history and culture of Paris.

# The Ghostly Woman of Oscar Wilde's Grave

THE LEGEND OF THE GHOSTLY woman who visits Oscar Wilde's grave has been circulating for decades. According to the story, a mysterious woman dressed in black would visit Wilde's grave each year on the anniversary of his death, leaving a single red rose as a tribute.

The woman's identity remains a mystery, with many speculating that she was a former lover or admirer of Wilde's. Others have suggested that she may have been a member of a secret society or cult, drawn to the cemetery by Wilde's connection to the occult.

Despite the many rumours and theories, the identity of the woman has never been definitively established. However, the legend lives on, with visitors to the cemetery still keeping an eye out for the mysterious figure in black.

Apart from the legend of the woman who visits Oscar Wilde's grave, there have been many other reported ghostly sightings and experiences in Père Lachaise. Some visitors have reported feeling an eerie presence or hearing unexplained noises, while others claim to have seen apparitions or experienced other supernatural phenomena.

One of the most famous alleged sightings occurred in 1999, when a group of tourists claimed to have seen a ghostly figure wearing 19th-century clothing walking through the cemetery. The sighting was captured on film and has since been analysed by paranormal experts, with opinions divided as to its authenticity.

Despite the lack of concrete evidence, the stories of ghostly encounters at Père Lachaise continue to captivate visitors and paranormal enthusiasts alike. Perhaps it is the sheer number of famous graves, or the cemetery's eerie atmosphere, that draws people to this place of mystery and intrigue.

## More Than Just Legends of Ghosts

BUT THERE IS MORE TO Père Lachaise than just ghostly legends. The cemetery is a place of great historical and cultural significance, and a stroll through its winding paths offers a glimpse into the past. From the ornate tombs of the wealthy and influential to the simple graves of the common people, Père Lachaise is a microcosm of French society and history.

One of the most striking features of the cemetery is its funerary art. The graves are adorned with sculptures, reliefs, and other decorative elements that reflect the artistic styles and trends of the time periods in which they were created. From neoclassical to art deco, the cemetery's funerary art offers a fascinating glimpse into the evolution of art and design over the past two centuries.

Another notable aspect of Père Lachaise is its role as a site of political and social history. Many of the graves are dedicated to figures who played key roles in French politics and society, from writers and philosophers to revolutionaries and resistance fighters. These graves serve as a reminder of the struggles and triumphs of the French people over the centuries, and of the important role that Père Lachaise has played in preserving their memory.

Overall, the Père Lachaise Cemetery is a place of great significance and intrigue, offering a unique glimpse into the past and a rich tapestry of stories to be uncovered. Whether you are interested in history, culture, or the paranormal, a visit to Père Lachaise is sure to be a memorable experience.

# EDWARD TURNER

# Chapter 4: The Hôtel de Sens

Paris is a city of stories, with a rich tapestry of history woven into every corner. Some of these stories are beautiful, inspiring, and awe-inspiring. Others are darker, filled with secrets, intrigue, and, of course, ghosts. One of the most haunted buildings in Paris is the Hôtel de Sens, a mediaeval mansion located in the Marais district.

## The History of the Hôtel de Sens

THE HÔTEL DE SENS WAS built in the late 15th century, and its story is one of evolution and transformation. Originally, the building was the residence of the archbishops of Sens, a town southeast of Paris. Over time, it passed into the hands of various noble families, including the notorious Guise family, before becoming a royal residence for the Queen Mother Catherine de' Medici.

During the French Revolution, the Hôtel de Sens was used as a prison. The building's elegant rooms were transformed into dungeons, and it became a place of great suffering and despair. After the Revolution, the building was sold to a baker, who used it as a bakery for almost a century. In the early 20th century, it was purchased by the city of Paris and turned into a public library.

Today, the Hôtel de Sens is the home of the Forney Library, a renowned repository of art and design resources. But despite its transformation over the centuries, the building's history has left its mark. It is said that the Hôtel de Sens is haunted by the ghosts of those who suffered within its walls.

## The Ghostly Young Woman

THE MOST FAMOUS GHOSTLY resident of the Hôtel de Sens is the young woman who is said to haunt the building to this day. According to legend, she was a noblewoman who fell in love with a commoner. Her family was outraged and locked her away in a tower within the Hôtel de Sens. The woman spent months locked in the tower, pining for her love and slowly losing her grip on reality. One day, she leapt from the tower to her death on the cobblestones below.

Since then, visitors to the Hôtel de Sens have claimed to see the ghostly figure of the young woman wandering the halls. Some say they have seen her in the library, while others claim to have spotted her image in mirrors or on photographs. Some visitors have even reported hearing her voice calling out for help.

## Other Ghostly Encounters

WHILE THE YOUNG WOMAN is the most famous ghost associated with the Hôtel de Sens, she is not the only spirit said to haunt the building. Visitors have reported hearing unexplained footsteps echoing through the halls, as well as mysterious knocks and bangs coming from empty rooms. Some have even reported feeling a cold, ghostly presence in certain areas of the building.

One popular story involves a woman who was alone in one of the library's reading rooms late one night. Suddenly, she heard the sound of a page turning in a nearby book. When she turned to investigate, she saw a pair of ghostly hands turning the pages of the book, even though no one was there. Terrified, she ran from the room and never returned.

Another visitor claimed to have seen a ghostly figure standing in one of the windows of the Hôtel de Sens, watching the street below. When they investigated, they found that the window was sealed shut and impossible to open.

## The Mystique of the Hôtel de Sens

DESPITE THE STORIES of ghostly sightings and experiences, not everyone believes in the supernatural. However, even those who are sceptical can't deny the allure of the Hôtel de Sens. The building's long and varied history, from its beginnings as a noble residence to its time as a prison and then a bakery, make it an intriguing and mysterious place. Its Gothic architecture, with its pointed arches and soaring spires, adds to its mystique and sense of foreboding.

For those who do believe in ghosts, the Hôtel de Sens is a place of great fascination. The stories of the young woman and other ghostly sightings have been passed down through generations of Parisians, adding to the building's haunted reputation. Some even claim that the spirits of those who suffered within its walls have been trapped there, unable to move on.

Regardless of whether you believe in ghosts or not, the Hôtel de Sens remains a captivating and eerie place. Its long and complex history has left its mark, and its ghostly reputation only adds to its intrigue. For those who are brave enough, a visit to the Hôtel de Sens is sure to be an unforgettable experience, filled with mystery and a sense of the unknown.

# GHOSTS OF PARIS: TEN HAUNTED PLACES IN THE CITY OF LOVE

# Chapter 5: The Hôtel de Ville

Paris is known for its rich history, stunning architecture, and romantic atmosphere. However, beneath its charming and delightful façade lies a darker side. Some parts of Paris are dark and eerie, with rumours of ghosts haunting certain buildings. The Hôtel de Ville, one of the most famous landmarks in Paris, is no exception. In this chapter, we will explore the history of the Hôtel de Ville, its significance during the French Revolution, the legend of the ghosts of the executed that are said to haunt the building, and other rumoured ghostly sightings and experiences.

The Hôtel de Ville, also known as the City Hall, is located in the heart of Paris. The original building was constructed in the 14th century and was used as the seat of the municipal government. The building was destroyed in 1871 during the Paris Commune, a political and social movement that took place after the Franco-Prussian War. The current building was constructed in the 19th century in the style of the Renaissance. The building has been renovated and restored several times throughout the years, adding to its rich and fascinating history.

The Hôtel de Ville has been the site of many significant events throughout French history. It has been the location of numerous official receptions, ceremonies, and celebrations. It has also hosted important political meetings and negotiations, making it a symbol of the country's democracy and governance.

# The French Revolution

DURING THE FRENCH REVOLUTION, the Hôtel de Ville played a significant role in this period. It was the headquarters of the Paris Commune, a revolutionary government that ruled Paris for two months in 1792. The building was also the site of the execution of many prominent figures, including King Louis XVI and Marie Antoinette. These events have left an indelible mark on the building's history, and many believe that the spirits of those executed still roam the halls to this day.

The Hôtel de Ville is said to be haunted by the ghosts of those executed during the French Revolution. It is said that the spirits of those who were executed in the building's courtyard still roam the halls, and some visitors claim to have seen the ghosts of the executed wandering the building. One famous ghostly legend associated with the Hôtel de Ville is that of Marie Antoinette's ghost. It is said that her ghost has been seen in the building, dressed in the clothes she wore on the day of her execution. Some people have reported feeling a cold breeze and hearing the sound of a woman's voice when they visit the building.

## Other Ghostly Sightings

APART FROM THE LEGEND of the ghosts of the executed, there are other rumoured ghostly sightings and experiences associated with the Hôtel de Ville. Some visitors claim to have seen shadowy figures moving through the halls or heard unexplained noises. Others report feeling a sense of unease or a feeling of being watched while in the building. These eerie occurrences have added to the building's reputation as one of the most haunted places in Paris.

Despite its dark and eerie reputation, the Hôtel de Ville remains one of the most iconic buildings in Paris. Its beautiful architecture and rich history continue to attract visitors from all over the world. The building has undergone significant renovations and restorations over the years, ensuring that it remains a symbol of the country's governance and democracy. However, its haunted history has also made it a must-visit destination for those interested in the darker side of Paris's history.

The Hôtel de Ville is a fascinating building with a rich and eerie history. Its significance during the French Revolution and its association with the ghosts of the executed have added to its reputation as one of the most haunted places in Paris. Whether you believe in ghosts or not, there is no denying the eerie atmosphere that surrounds the Hôtel de Ville. Its dark past, combined with its stunning architecture and central location, make it a popular destination for tourists and history enthusiasts alike. Despite the rumours and legends, the building remains an important symbol of French democracy and governance. So if you find yourself in Paris, don't miss the chance to explore the Hôtel de Ville and uncover its haunted history for yourself.

# EDWARD TURNER

42

# Chapter 6: The Palace of Versailles

The Palace of Versailles is one of the most recognizable landmarks in France, known for its opulent beauty and rich history. It served as the official residence of the kings and queens of France from 1682 until the French Revolution in 1789. It is not surprising that a place with such a long and tumultuous history is said to be haunted by the ghosts of its past. In this chapter, we will explore the legends and stories surrounding the Palace of Versailles, and the ghostly apparitions that are said to haunt its halls.

## History and Significance of the Palace of Versailles

THE PALACE OF VERSAILLES was originally built as a hunting lodge for Louis XIII in the early 17th century. It was expanded by his son, Louis XIV, who transformed it into a grand palace that would become a symbol of his power and prestige. Over the years, the palace was expanded and renovated by subsequent kings and queens, each adding their own touches to the building's already impressive architecture.

The palace played a significant role in French history, particularly during the reign of Louis XIV. He transformed the palace into a centre of French power and culture, hosting lavish parties and events that were attended by the most important people in France. It was during this time that the Hall of Mirrors was constructed, which is said to be one of the most haunted areas of the palace.

# Legend of the Ghosts of Louis XVI and Marie Antoinette

THE TRAGIC FATE OF Louis XVI and Marie Antoinette has contributed to the legends and stories of their ghosts haunting the Palace of Versailles. Louis XVI was the last king of France before the French Revolution, and he and his queen were both executed by guillotine during the Reign of Terror in 1793.

Reports of their ghostly apparitions began to emerge shortly after their deaths. Many have claimed to have seen the ghost of Marie Antoinette in the Hall of Mirrors, the Queen's Bedchamber, and the Petit Trianon. Some have reported seeing her wandering through the palace gardens, often accompanied by the sound of her ghostly footsteps.

The ghost of Louis XVI has also been reported throughout the palace, particularly in the Royal Chapel and the Salon d'Hercule. Some visitors have even claimed to have heard his voice calling out for his queen.

# Other Rumoured Ghostly Sightings and Experiences

IN ADDITION TO THE ghosts of Louis XVI and Marie Antoinette, there are many other reports of ghostly sightings and experiences at the Palace of Versailles. The gardens and grounds are said to be particularly haunted, with reports of ghostly carriages, the ghostly woman in black, and even a ghostly dog.

The ghostly carriage is said to appear on certain nights, drawn by a team of spectral horses. It is said to be the carriage that transported the body of Louis XVIII from the palace to his final resting place. The ghostly woman in black is said to appear near the Grand Canal, dressed in mourning clothes and weeping for her lost love.

The Palace of Versailles is not only a symbol of French power and prestige, but also a place of mystery and intrigue. Its rich history and stunning architecture have made it one of the most visited tourist attractions in France, and its legends and stories of ghostly hauntings have only added to its allure. The stories of the ghosts of Louis XVI and Marie Antoinette, and the other rumoured sightings and experiences, continue to fascinate visitors to this day. Whether you believe in ghosts or not, the Palace of Versailles is a place that is steeped in history, beauty, and mystery.

# Chapter 7: The Château de Châteaubriant

The Château de Châteaubriant is an awe-inspiring fortress that is nestled in the town of Châteaubriant in western France. This magnificent castle was initially constructed in the 11th century as a simple wooden fortification by the Lords of Châteaubriant. Over the years, it underwent many renovations and reconstructions until it became the grand chateau that we know and love today.

In the 13th century, the wooden fortress was reconstructed into a magnificent stone chateau, which became home to many noble families over the centuries. The Lords of Châteaubriant, the Montmorency family, and the La Trémoille family all called this castle their home at one point in time. The chateau played a significant role in the region's history, serving as a military stronghold during the Hundred Years War and being occupied by English troops in the 14th century.

The 16th century was a tumultuous time for the castle and the region as a whole, as it became a centre of the French Wars of Religion. During the French Revolution, the state seized the chateau and turned it into a prison. Today, the chateau is a historic monument that attracts tourists from all over the world.

EDWARD TURNER

# Ghostly Sightings at the Château

APART FROM ITS RICH history, the Château de Châteaubriant is also renowned for its supernatural occurrences and ghostly sightings. The ghost of Françoise de Foix, a noblewoman who lived during the 16th century, is said to haunt the castle. Françoise was the mistress of King Francis I and was known for her beauty and intelligence. However, her relationship with the king caused envy and resentment among the courtiers, and after the king's death, she was exiled to Châteaubriant.

Françoise lived at the chateau for many years, but she was never happy there. She was isolated and lonely, and her health deteriorated. She died at the chateau in 1537, and since then, her ghost is said to haunt the castle. Many people have reported seeing her ghostly figure wandering through the halls of the chateau, and some claim to have heard her whispering in their ears.

Apart from the ghost of Françoise de Foix, there are many other rumours of supernatural occurrences at the Château de Châteaubriant. Visitors have reported seeing ghostly apparitions in the castle's courtyard, and some have claimed to hear unexplained noises and footsteps in the castle's empty halls. Some even claim to have seen the ghost of a young girl who died at the chateau many years ago.

The castle's many ghost stories have made it a popular destination for paranormal enthusiasts and history buffs alike. Despite the centuries that have passed since Françoise's death, her ghostly presence still lingers in the castle's halls, reminding us of the castle's past and its many stories.

# Architecture and Designs

THE CHÂTEAU DE CHÂTEAUBRIANT is not only a historic monument but also a fascinating place to visit for anyone who's interests lay outside of the supernatural. The castle's impressive architecture and intricate designs are a testament to the skill and craftsmanship of the builders who constructed it. The chateau's rich history and the legends of its ghosts make it a captivating destination for anyone looking to immerse themselves in the past.

The castle's imposing walls and majestic towers are a reminder of its former military strength, while the ghost stories add an element of mystery and intrigue that is sure to captivate anyone's imagination. Whether you are a history buff, a paranormal enthusiast, or simply someone who appreciates fine architecture, the Château de Châteaubriant is a must-visit destination that will leave you breathless.

The Château de Châteaubriant is a truly magnificent castle that has stood the test of time. From its humble beginnings as a wooden fortification to its current status as a historic monument, the chateau has seen centuries of history and witnessed some of the most significant events in the region.

However, what truly sets the Château de Châteaubriant apart are the ghostly tales that surround it. The ghost of Françoise de Foix and the other supernatural occurrences at the chateau make it a unique destination for anyone interested in the paranormal. The chateau's ghost stories add an element of mystery and intrigue that is sure to capture the imagination of anyone who visits.

Whether you are a history buff or a paranormal enthusiast, the Château de Châteaubriant is an awe-inspiring destination that is worth a visit. The castle's rich history, impressive architecture, and legends of ghosts combine to make it a truly unforgettable experience.

# GHOSTS OF PARIS: TEN HAUNTED PLACES IN THE CITY OF LOVE

# Chapter 8: The Musée de la Chasse et de la Nature

The Musée de la Chasse et de la Nature, or the Museum of Hunting and Nature, is a Parisian gem that offers a fascinating look into the relationship between humans and animals throughout history. The museum is housed in the Hôtel de Guénégaud, a stunning 17th-century building in the Marais district of Paris that served as the residence of the Duke of Guénégaud before it was acquired by the French government and used as a school in the 19th century.

Founded in 1964 by Francois and Jacqueline Sommer, the Musée de la Chasse et de la Nature is a testament to the Sommers' passion for hunting and nature-related art and artefacts. Their extensive collection, which includes paintings, sculptures, taxidermy, and other objects, has been curated to offer visitors a glimpse into the rich history of hunting and the role it has played in our relationship with nature.

The museum's exhibits are arranged thematically, taking visitors on a journey through time to explore topics such as the evolution of hunting techniques, the art of taxidermy, and the representation of animals in art. One of the most interesting exhibits is dedicated to the role of animals in society, showcasing how they have been used for transportation, entertainment, and companionship throughout history.

Visitors can also marvel at the museum's permanent collection, which includes works by some of the most renowned artists in history. Jean-Baptiste Oudry's striking animal portraits, Edgar Degas' impressionist paintings of horses, and Pablo Picasso's lithographs of bulls are just a few of the highlights.

# Rumoured Hauntings

BUT THE MUSÉE DE LA Chasse et de la Nature is not just a celebration of our relationship with animals; it is also rumoured to be haunted. According to legend, the ghost of Jean-Jacques Rousseau, the famous philosopher and nature lover, haunts the museum.

Rousseau was a prominent figure in 18th-century France, known for his works on politics, education, and the nature of humanity. His writings often reflected his appreciation for the natural world, and it is said that his ghost roams the halls of the Musée de la Chasse et de la Nature because of his love for animals and nature.

Some visitors have reported seeing a ghostly figure that resembles Rousseau wandering through the exhibits, stopping to admire the taxidermy animals and artwork. The legend of Rousseau's ghost only adds to the allure of the museum, attracting curious visitors who want to experience the museum's eerie atmosphere for themselves.

But the stories of hauntings don't stop with Rousseau's ghost. There have been other rumoured ghostly sightings and experiences at the Musée de la Chasse et de la Nature. Some visitors have reported feeling a sense of unease or being watched while in the museum, while others have claimed to see shadowy figures or hear strange noises.

One popular story involves a group of visitors who were exploring the museum's basement. They reported feeling a sudden drop in temperature and hearing strange whispers, as though there were unseen voices speaking to them. When they attempted to leave the basement, they found that the door was stuck and would not open. After several minutes of trying to force the door open, it suddenly swung open on its own, allowing them to leave.

# A Deep History of Hunting

DESPITE THE RUMOURS of hauntings, the Musée de la Chasse et de la Nature remains a must-visit destination for anyone interested in the history of hunting and the relationship between humans and animals. The museum's extensive collection and thematic exhibits offer a unique perspective on our relationship with nature and the role that hunting has played in our society.

As you walk through the museum's halls, taking in the beautiful artwork and artefacts, you may feel a sense of unease, wondering if you are truly alone or if there are unseen spirits watching you. But perhaps this is part of the magic of the Musée de la Chasse et de la Nature, where the line between the past and present, reality and legend, is blurred.

Whether you believe in ghosts or not, a visit to the Musée de la Chasse et de la Nature is sure to be an unforgettable experience. As you immerse yourself in the museum's exhibits, you will gain a deeper understanding of our complex relationship with animals and the natural world. And who knows, you may even catch a glimpse of the famous philosopher's ghostly apparition as you wander through the halls.

# GHOSTS OF PARIS: TEN HAUNTED PLACES IN THE CITY OF LOVE

# Chapter 9: The Sainte-Chapelle

The city of Paris is home to some of the most beautiful and historically significant structures in the world, and one of the most impressive is the Sainte-Chapelle. This stunning Gothic chapel has a long and fascinating history that spans centuries, and it is said to be home to a number of ghostly legends and sightings.

## History and Architecture of the Sainte-Chapelle

THE SAINTE-CHAPELLE was built in the 13th century by King Louis IX to house his collection of Christian relics, including the Crown of Thorns. The chapel was designed by Pierre de Montreuil, one of the most important architects of his time, and construction began in 1242. It was completed in just seven years, which is a remarkable feat considering the complexity of the design and the fact that it was built entirely by hand.

The Sainte-Chapelle is located on the Île de la Cité, a small island in the heart of Paris. The chapel is divided into two levels, with the lower level being used as a parish church and the upper level being used for private worship by the king and his court. The upper chapel is the most impressive part of the building, with soaring stained-glass windows that stretch from the floor to the ceiling.

The stained-glass windows are the most striking feature of the Sainte-Chapelle, and they are some of the most beautiful and intricate examples of Gothic art in the world. The windows depict scenes from the Old and New Testaments, as well as from the lives of the saints. The glass is arranged in such a way that it creates a stunning effect of light and colour, with the sun streaming through the windows and casting a rainbow of hues across the chapel.

## Legend of the Ghostly Knight

LIKE MANY OLD BUILDINGS in Paris, the Sainte-Chapelle has its share of ghostly legends and stories. One of the most famous is the legend of the ghostly knight. According to the legend, the knight was a soldier who died in battle and was buried in the chapel. His ghost is said to wander the upper chapel, clad in his armour and carrying a sword.

There are many versions of the story of the ghostly knight, but one of the most popular is that he is the ghost of a Crusader who fought in the Holy Land. According to the story, the knight died in battle and was brought back to Paris by his fellow soldiers, who buried him in the Sainte-Chapelle. His ghost is said to be restless, and he wanders the chapel at night, searching for peace.

## Other Ghostly Sightings and Experiences

IN ADDITION TO THE ghostly knight, there have been many other sightings and experiences reported in the Sainte-Chapelle over the years. Some people claim to have seen ghostly apparitions or heard strange noises, while others have reported feeling a sense of unease or fear when inside the chapel.

One of the most famous ghost stories associated with the Sainte-Chapelle is that of a group of Russian visitors who were taking a tour of the chapel. According to the story, the visitors were approached by a woman who was dressed in old-fashioned clothing and who spoke to them in French. The visitors were surprised that the woman spoke French so well, and they asked her where she was from. She replied that she was from Russia, and when they asked her how she came to speak French so well, she told them that she had lived in France for many years.

The visitors were intrigued by the woman and asked her name, but she simply smiled and disappeared. When they later asked the staff at the chapel about the woman, they were told that no one fitting her description worked there, and that there were no other explanations for her sudden appearance and disappearance. This has led many to believe that the ghostly woman is indeed the spirit of Isabelle of France, making a visit to her cherished chapel.

While some may be sceptical of ghostly encounters such as these, it is clear that the Sainte-Chapelle has a long and fascinating history that continues to captivate visitors to this day. From its origins as a royal chapel, to its use as a storage facility and restoration project, to its current status as a popular tourist attraction, the Sainte-Chapelle has seen it all. And with the ghostly knight and mysterious woman adding to its mystique, it is sure to remain a beloved and enigmatic destination for years to come.

# EDWARD TURNER

62

# Chapter 10: The Place des Vosges

Paris is a city steeped in history and culture, with many beautiful and historic sites that attract visitors from all over the world. One such site is the Place des Vosges, located in the heart of the Marais district. This square is one of the oldest and most beautiful in Paris, with a rich history that dates back to the 17th century.

Originally known as the Place Royale, the square was built during the reign of King Henry IV, who wanted to create a grand and impressive square to showcase his power and wealth. The square was designed by the architect Baptiste du Cerceau, who also worked on the Louvre, and was the first planned square in Paris. It quickly became a popular gathering place for the city's elite, who would come to enjoy the beautiful gardens and elegant architecture.

Over the years, the Place des Vosges has played an important role in the city's history. During the French Revolution, it was the site of many executions, including that of Charlotte Corday, who assassinated the radical journalist Jean-Paul Marat. Today, the square is home to many museums, art galleries, and boutiques, as well as a number of high-end apartments.

## Ghostly Sightings Within the Square

DESPITE ITS BEAUTY and elegance, the Place des Vosges has a darker side, with many ghost stories associated with the square.

According to legend, the ghosts of those executed during the French Revolution still haunt the square to this day. Visitors have reported seeing spectral figures dressed in the clothing of the era walking through the gardens and along the arcades that surround the square.

One of the most famous ghost stories associated with the Place des Vosges involves the execution of Charlotte Corday. According to legend, her ghost appears on the anniversary of her execution, dressed in the white dress she wore to her execution. She is said to walk through the square and disappear near the spot where she was executed.

Other ghostly sightings and experiences have been reported in the square as well. Some visitors have reported feeling a sense of unease or being watched while walking through the square, while others have reported hearing strange noises or feeling a sudden drop in temperature.

One particularly eerie experience involved a group of tourists who were visiting the square late at night. As they were walking through the gardens, they suddenly heard the sound of hooves on the pavement. When they turned around, they saw a ghostly figure riding a horse through the square. The figure disappeared as suddenly as it had appeared, leaving the tourists shaken and bewildered.

## A Popular Historical Destination

DESPITE THE MANY GHOST stories associated with the Place des Vosges, the square remains a popular destination for visitors to Paris. Whether you're interested in history, architecture, or simply enjoying a relaxing afternoon in a beautiful setting, the Place des Vosges is a must-see destination that is sure to leave a lasting impression. And who knows, you might even catch a glimpse of a ghost or two while you're there!

In addition to its historic significance and ghostly legends, the Place des Vosges is also known for its stunning architecture and picturesque gardens. The square is surrounded by elegant 17th-century buildings, each with its own unique features and charm. The gardens are beautifully maintained and offer a peaceful escape from the bustling city streets.

If you're interested in history, there are many museums and galleries in the square that are worth a visit. The Maison de Victor Hugo is located on the square and is dedicated to the life and work of the famous writer. The Musée Carnavalet is also nearby and offers a fascinating look at the history of Paris.

## There's Always Shopping

FOR THOSE WHO ENJOY shopping, the Place des Vosges is home to many high-end boutiques and shops. You can find everything from designer clothing to handmade jewellery and unique souvenirs.

Finally, the square is also home to a number of excellent restaurants and cafes, making it the perfect place to relax and enjoy a meal or a cup of coffee. The outdoor terraces are particularly popular during the warmer months, offering a perfect vantage point for people-watching and enjoying the beautiful surroundings.

Overall, the Place des Vosges is a destination that offers something for everyone. Whether you're interested in history, architecture, shopping, or simply enjoying a peaceful afternoon in a beautiful setting, this square is not to be missed. And who knows, you might even catch a glimpse of a ghost or two while you're there!

# GHOSTS OF PARIS: TEN HAUNTED PLACES IN THE CITY OF LOVE

# Conclusion

Paris is a city that never ceases to amaze. With its grand architecture, vibrant culture, and rich history, the City of Light has been a source of inspiration for generations of artists, writers, and thinkers. But beneath its beauty and sophistication lies a darker side, one that is steeped in mystery and legend.

As we come to the end of our journey through the haunted places of Paris, we cannot help but marvel at the city's rich history and the stories that have been passed down through generations. From the grandest palaces to the smallest alleys, Paris is a city that is steeped in ghostly tales and spooky legends.

In this book, we have explored ten of the most rumoured haunted places in Paris, each with its own unique story to tell. We have delved into the history and significance of each location and shared the legends of the ghosts that are said to haunt them. But our exploration does not end here, as there are countless other places in Paris that are said to be haunted and waiting to be discovered.

The Palace of Versailles, for instance, is a place that is known for its grandeur and opulence, but it is also a place that is steeped in ghostly tales. The legends of the ghosts of Louis XVI and Marie Antoinette, for instance, have been the subject of countless books and films, and continue to be a source of fascination for many.

But it is not just the grand palaces that are rumoured to be haunted in Paris. The Musée de la Chasse et de la Nature, for instance, may not be as famous as other museums in Paris, but its connection to Jean-Jacques Rousseau has made it a popular destination for those interested in the supernatural.

As we have seen, some of these stories are more well-known than others. The Eiffel Tower, for example, is not typically associated with ghostly sightings, but as we have learned, it has its own haunting tale to tell. Meanwhile, the Place des Vosges is a beautiful square that is said to be haunted by the ghosts of the past.

Of course, some may argue that these stories are nothing more than fanciful tales, exaggerated over time and with little basis in fact. And it is true that many of these legends have been embellished over the years, perhaps to make them more interesting or to add to their mystique. But regardless of their veracity, these stories serve an important purpose in our cultural consciousness. They remind us of our connection to the past and the ways in which our shared history can continue to shape our present.

The legends of the haunted places in Paris add to the allure of the city. For centuries, Paris has been known as the City of Light, a beacon of culture and sophistication that has drawn people from around the world. But the ghostly tales that are associated with the city add an extra layer of mystique, giving Paris an almost otherworldly quality that has captured the imaginations of people for generations.

# GHOSTS OF PARIS: TEN HAUNTED PLACES IN THE CITY OF LOVE

As we close this book, we encourage you to continue exploring the haunted places of Paris for yourself. While we have shared some of the most well-known stories, there are countless other legends and rumours waiting to be discovered. Take a stroll through the winding alleyways of Montmartre or explore the catacombs beneath the city. Who knows what secrets and stories you may uncover?

In the end, the ghosts of Paris are not simply the stuff of legend. They are a reminder of the city's rich history and its ongoing connection to the past. As long as we continue to tell their stories, they will continue to haunt us, and to remind us of the magic and mystery that lies at the heart of this remarkable city. Paris truly is a city that never ceases to amaze, and the ghosts that are said to haunt its streets and buildings are just one aspect of its fascinating history and culture.

Whether you are a believer in the supernatural or not, there is something undeniably compelling about the stories of the haunted places of Paris. They remind us of the power of storytelling and the ways in which our imaginations can be captured by the mysteries and legends of the past.

So the next time you find yourself in Paris, take some time to explore the haunted places of the city. Whether you are wandering the halls of a grand palace or venturing down a quiet alleyway, you never know what ghostly tales you may encounter.

And who knows, you may just come away from your journey with a deeper appreciation for the history and culture of this remarkable city. Paris truly is a city that never ceases to amaze, and its ghosts are just one part of the magic that makes it such a captivating destination.

---

THANK YOU FOR TAKING the time to explore the haunted history of Paris with me. It has been a pleasure to share these stories with you and to delve into the mysterious and eerie side of this beautiful city. I hope that this book has inspired you to explore Paris in a different way, and to seek out the ghosts and legends that continue to haunt its streets.

I would like to extend a special thanks to all those who shared their personal experiences and knowledge of these haunted places, as well as to the staff at the various locations for their hospitality and support. Finally, I would like to thank you, the reader, for joining me on this journey into the supernatural.

Happy ghost hunting!

# Don't miss out!

Visit the website below and you can sign up to receive emails whenever Edward Turner publishes a new book. There's no charge and no obligation.

https://books2read.com/r/B-A-SYIZ-CYJLC

# Also by Edward Turner

# About the Author

Edward Turner is a renowned author who specializes in exploring the realms of ghosts, the paranormal, and cryptids. With a captivating writing style and an insatiable curiosity for the unknown, Turner has garnered a dedicated following of readers who are captivated by his thrilling and eerie tales.

Born with an innate fascination for the supernatural, Turner has spent decades delving into the depths of paranormal phenomena, unearthing captivating stories and untangling mysteries that lie beyond the veil of the ordinary. His extensive research and meticulous attention to detail have earned him a reputation as a leading authority in the field.

Through his books, Turner expertly weaves together chilling accounts of encounters with ghosts, offering readers a glimpse into the ethereal world that coexists alongside our own. His ability to paint vivid portraits of spectral apparitions and convey the haunting atmosphere of haunted locations has made his works both spine-tingling and thought-provoking.

Turner's exploration of the paranormal doesn't stop at ghosts. He also dives into the fascinating world of cryptids—creatures that defy conventional explanation. His in-depth investigations into legendary creatures such as Bigfoot, the Loch Ness Monster, and the Chupacabra showcase his commitment to shedding light on these enigmatic beings.

With each page, Edward Turner's readers are drawn deeper into the enigmatic and unknown. His unique storytelling ability combined with his meticulous research has made him a sought-after author for those with an insatiable thirst for the supernatural. Whether delving into ghostly encounters or unraveling the mysteries of elusive cryptids, Turner's books offer a spine-chilling and immersive reading experience that leaves readers questioning the boundaries of our reality.

Edward Turner's works have earned critical acclaim and numerous accolades within the paranormal genre. He continues to explore the unexplained, captivating readers with his distinctive narrative style and unwavering dedication to unveiling the mysteries that lie hidden in the shadows.